The Ladder to Life

Every Step Counts When God Holds The Ladder

BY

Ugochi A. Ibekwe (Yoursoluriter)

PROLOGUE

There comes a moment in every life when the soul begins to stir, asking questions the world cannot answer:

Why am I here? Where do I go from here? Is there more to life than this?

This book was born out of that sacred search. Not from comfort, but from wilderness. Not from answers, but from the hunger to know God beyond religion—deeply, intimately, and truthfully.

"The Ladder to Life" is not a quick fix, nor is it a manual for perfection. It is a journey—a climb—through valleys of brokenness, up mountains of revelation, and into the arms of a God who sees, knows, and loves us still. Like Jacob in the wilderness, I too wrestled with God. I too saw the ladder stretch from Earth to Heaven, where angels ascended and descended, reminding me that life is not random—it's divine.

Each chapter is a rung on that ladder. A step closer to wholeness. A step higher in faith. A step deeper into truth. If you have ever felt like giving up, like your soul was too tired to keep climbing, this book was written for you.

My prayer is that these pages will not just speak to your mind, but minister to your spirit. That you will encounter the living God—not just in theology or tradition—but in transformation.

This is my testimony. This is my offering. This is "The Ladder to Life".

ACKNOWLEDGEMENT

First and foremost, I give all glory, honor, and praise to God Almighty, the Author and Finisher of my faith. Without His divine guidance, presence, and unshakable love, this book would not have been possible.

The Ladder to Life was birthed through prayer, tears, revelation, and divine encounters that only He could orchestrate. It is my offering to His Kingdom, a testament to His grace, and a beacon of hope to those still climbing.

To my spiritual mentor and dear brother, Valerian Chibueze Okoye, thank you for your immeasurable support, wisdom, and unwavering belief in this assignment. Your mentorship breathed life into these pages.

Your words of encouragement and leadership stirred my spirit when I felt like giving up. You didn't just coach me through writing—you walked with me as a guide led by the Holy Spirit. I am forever grateful for your obedience to God's calling on your life.

To every reader who picks up this book, may it draw you closer to the One who holds your purpose, your healing, and your victory which is EL-SHADDAI God Almighty. May each chapter lead you one rung higher in your spiritual journey. This is more than a book—it's an invitation to climb.

All for His glory.

With love and deep gratitude,

Ugochi A. Ibekwe (Yoursoulriter)

DEDICATION

To **Yahweh, the Ancient of Days, El Roi, Elo-him** My Abba, My Sustainer, My Eternal Source. Before I formed the words, You planted them in my spirit. Before I saw the vision, You whispered it in the secret place.

This book is not merely written by me—it is breathed through me by You.

I cast this offering like oil at Your feet, for You are the Ladder and the Life. Be glorified in every line, every lesson, every life it touches. Let Your Spirit move through these pages as fire, as wind, as living water.

To **every soul in the wilderness**, those who cry out behind closed doors, those who war in the unseen realms—this is your reminder: You are not invisible to Heaven.
Your tears have been bottled. Your climb is not in vain. You are ascending, even when it feels like you're falling. May this book be a balm for your wounds, a trumpet to your dry bones, and a compass back to the heart of the Father.

To **Valerian Chibueze Okoye**, a divine appointment in human form.

Thank you for sharpening the iron of my purpose and for standing in the gap with prophetic precision.

Your mentorship did not just guide my pen—it ignited my calling.

You are a true oracle of the Kingdom, and your obedience has birthed legacy in others.

To **the generations yet unborn**, those who will walk in both the light of promise and the shadows of trial— May you hunger for truth, not trend. May you seek the voice of God above the noise of man. And when the world tells you to settle, may you always choose the climb.

Let *The Ladder to Life* be your inheritance, a spiritual map that leads not just to success, but to surrender. May you rise on the wings of righteousness, anchored in grace, ablaze with purpose, and wrapped in the fear of the Lord.

In Jesus' name—Amen.

Table of Contents

CHAPTER 1:

GOD'S LOVE FOR MAN

"God is love" is written upon every opening bud, upon every blade of springing grass. The birds of the air, filling the world with their joyful songs, the delicately tinted flowers perfuming the breeze, and the lofty trees of the forest with their rich, living green—all testify to the tender, fatherly care of our God and His desire to make His children happy.

Nature reveals the boundless love of God. Consider the beauty and wonder of the natural world, marvelously adapted to the needs and happiness of not only humanity but all living creatures. The sunshine and rain that gladden and refresh the earth, the hills, seas, and plains—all speak of the Creator's love. God supplies the daily needs of His creation, both human and animal.

When God created man, He made him perfect in His image, as though fresh from the Creator's hand. Yet, after man's fall, it is written that God cursed the ground for man's sake (Genesis 3:17). Even in this, nature carries messages of hope and comfort. Flowers bloom among thistles, and thorns are adorned with roses, revealing God's love and mercy.

God's character shines through His infinite love and compassion. When Moses prayed, "Show me thy glory," the Lord answered, "I will make all my goodness pass before thee" (Exodus 33:18-19). As the Lord passed before Moses, He proclaimed, "The Lord, the Lord God, merciful and gracious, longsuffering, and abundant in goodness and truth, keeping mercy for thousands, forgiving iniquity and transgression and sin" (Exodus 34:6-7). He is slow to anger and delights in mercy (Jonah 4:2; Micah 7:18).

The ultimate expression of God's love is found in the sacrifice of His Son: "For God so loved the world that He gave His only begotten Son, that whosoever believeth in Him should not perish, but have everlasting life" (John 3:16). Out of His boundless love, God offered His Son to save humanity. Christ came to manifest the Father's love, declaring, "The Lord hath anointed me to preach the gospel to the poor; He hath sent me to heal the brokenhearted, to preach deliverance to the captives, and recovering of sight to the blind, to set at liberty them that are bruised" (Luke 4:18).

Jesus went about doing good, healing all who were oppressed by Satan. Entire villages were freed from sickness because of His touch. His life radiated divine love, mercy, and compassion. The poorest and humblest were not afraid to approach Him, and even little children found rest in His presence, gazing into His face, gentle and radiant with love. He promised, "Peace I leave with you, my peace I give unto you: not as the world giveth, give I unto you" (John 14:27). Our hearts remain restless until they find rest in God.

God's promises are sure, and He cannot lie. He vows to rescue us from every temptation, and we must trust in His faithfulness. Allow me to share a testimony that illustrates God's protection in the face of danger.

While living in a dormitory in Nigeria, I often studied in the exam hall, a quiet place away from the classroom but within the school premises. One day, feeling weak but needing to prepare for an upcoming exam, I brought my Bible to the hall. After reading and praying, I decided to take a short nap. What felt like an hour stretched longer, and I was awakened by an unsettling silence. The others who had been studying with me had left, and I was alone. An inner prompting urged me to look under my seat, where, to my shock, I saw a colorful snake. Immediately, I stood, pleaded the blood of Jesus, and hurried out of the hall.

As I walked to lunch, I reflected on what could have happened—being bitten, hospitalized, or worse. Yet, God's promise came to mind: "I have given you authority to trample on snakes and scorpions and to overcome all the power of the enemy; nothing will harm you" (Luke 10:19). God, the Faithful Father, always protects His sheep, showing up at the right time to prove His love. He never fails when we need Him most.

Do not be misled, for your soul's sake. Trust in God's protection and strive to avoid the path where "the fire is not quenched, and the worm does not die" (Mark 9:44). If you mingle with the careless who jest about eternal matters, you risk becoming their instrument and may even blame God in your distress. Play your part, and our merciful God will protect you.

The Father's love for us is not because of Christ's sacrifice but the reason for it. Christ was the medium through which God poured His infinite love upon a fallen world. "God was in Christ, reconciling the world unto Himself" (2 Corinthians 5:19).

In the agony of Gethsemane and the death on Calvary, the heart of infinite love paid the price of our redemption.

Jesus said, "Therefore doth my Father love me, because I lay down my life, that I might take it again" (John 10:17). In other words, "My Father loves you so much that He loves me even more for giving my life to redeem you." By becoming our substitute, taking our liabilities and transgressions, Christ endeared Himself to the Father. Through His sacrifice, God remains just while justifying those who believe in Jesus. Only the Son, who dwelt in the Father's bosom, could reveal the height, depth, and breadth of God's love.

The apostle John, overwhelmed by the greatness of this love, exclaimed, "Behold, what manner of love the

Father hath bestowed upon us, that we should be called the sons of God" (1 John 3:1). Through faith in Christ's atoning sacrifice, the sons of Adam become sons of God. By taking on human nature, Christ elevates humanity, making us worthy of the name "sons of God."

This love is unparalleled, unbreakable, and given to those who did not first love Him. In John 18:10, when Peter cut off Malchus' ear, Christ, in His loving kindness, restored it. Praise God! Because of His love, we are called to worship Him. Worship connects our hearts to His and is the most important act we can perform. God created the earth for man, not man for the earth. He calls us to serve Him to save our souls.

Prayer and work go hand in hand. God says, "Pray and work, and I will bless your efforts." Prayer without work is insufficient, and work without prayer is incomplete. Those who refuse to work are unworthy of God's gifts, for "if any would not work, neither should he eat" (2 Thessalonians 3:10).

When you pray, lift your hands toward heaven, not downward, and do not merely clasp them. As it is said, "Life without prayer goes out like a candle, and the soul becomes dead in God's eyes." His love endures forever. Amen.

CHAPTER 2:

GENUINE CONVERSION AND PENANCE

Conversion marks the beginning of a transformative relationship with God, an indispensable experience of His grace. Through faith in Jesus Christ, God forgives the repentant sinner, turning them from a life of guilt and condemnation into one filled with the peace and joy of salvation. This believer develops a genuine hatred for sin and a love for righteousness, walking in God's ways and forsaking the paths of self and the world. With their whole heart, they seek to know God's Word and prayerfully strive to obey His revelations.

A truly converted person refuses to be defiled by past sinful habits, evil associations, idolatrous practices, worldly festivals, or the works of the flesh. By God's sustaining grace and power, they remain separated from all forms of defilement. As Jesus said, "He who truly serves Me will plan to sin no more, for if you intend to walk with Me, you must carry My cross" (cf. Matthew 16:24).

How can a person be justified before God? How can a sinner become righteous? Only through Christ can we be brought into harmony with God and holiness. On the Day of Pentecost, convicted of their sin, the multitude cried out, "What shall we do?" Peter's first response was,

"Repent" (Acts 2:37-38). Later, he declared, "Repent and be converted, that your sins may be blotted out" (Acts 3:19). Genuine conversion involves sorrow for sin and a decisive turning away from it. We cannot renounce sin until we recognize its sinfulness, and without a heartfelt rejection of sin, there will be no real change in our lives.

Many misunderstand the nature of true conversion. It is a resolute, forward-moving journey with no return to sin. Consider Balaam, who, terrified by an angel with a drawn sword, acknowledged his guilt to save his life but showed no genuine repentance, no change of purpose, and no abhorrence of evil (Numbers 22:22-34). Similarly, Judas Iscariot, after betraying Jesus, exclaimed, "I have sinned in that I have betrayed the innocent blood" (Matthew 27:4). His confession was driven by fear of condemnation and judgment, not by deep, heartfelt grief for betraying the spotless Son of God.

In contrast, King David exemplifies true repentance after his fall. His conversion was sincere and profound, with no attempt to excuse his guilt or escape judgment. David saw the enormity of his transgression, loathed his sin, and longed for purity of heart and restoration to communion with God. His heartfelt prayer in Psalm 51:1-14 reflects this deep sorrow and desire for holiness. Such conversion is beyond human power; it comes only from Christ, the Creator of heaven and earth.

Some believe they must repent before coming to Christ, thinking repentance prepares them for forgiveness. While repentance precedes forgiveness—for only a broken and contrite heart feels the need for a Savior—it is not an obstacle between the sinner and Jesus. Scripture invites, "Come unto me, all ye that labour and are heavy laden, and I will give you rest" (Matthew 11:28). The virtue that flows from Christ leads to genuine repentance. Jesus declared, "I, if I be lifted up from the earth, will draw all men unto me" (John 12:32). As the sinner beholds Christ, the Lamb of God dying for the sins of the world, the mystery of redemption unfolds, and God's goodness leads to repentance. Christ's incomprehensible love, displayed on the cross, softens the heart, impresses the mind, and inspires contrition in the soul.

Even before sinners are fully aware of Christ's drawing, they may feel ashamed of their ways and abandon some evil habits. This is the power of Christ at work, quickening the conscience and amending the outward life. As Christ draws them to His cross, where their sins pierced Him, the commandments convict their conscience. The wickedness of their lives and the deep-seated sin of their souls are revealed. They begin to grasp Christ's righteousness and exclaim, "What is sin, that it required such a sacrifice for redemption? Was all this love, suffering, and humiliation necessary so we might not perish but have everlasting life?" Jesus likened entering the kingdom to a camel passing through the eye of a needle (Matthew 19:24), emphasizing that we must surrender pride and worldly wealth to follow Him. We are called to suffer with Him now to share in His eternal glory.

The Apostle Paul, though outwardly "blameless" in keeping the law (Philippians 3:6), saw himself as a sinner when he discerned the law's spiritual nature. He wrote, "I was alive without the law once: but when the commandment came, sin revived, and I died" (Romans 7:9). Recognizing the law's holy precepts, he saw sin's true hideousness and his self-esteem vanished. While human judgment may deem some sins trivial, God sees all sin as serious, for no sin is small in His sight. He evaluates all things as they truly are.

Beware of procrastination. Delaying repentance and the pursuit of purity through Jesus is a grave danger, one that has led countless souls to eternal loss. Sin, however small it seems, can only be indulged at the peril of infinite loss. What we do not overcome will overcome us and lead to our destruction. Jesus is ready to free us from sin, but He does not force the will. If we persist in transgression and reject His grace, we destroy ourselves. Scripture warns, "Behold, now is the accepted time; behold, now is the day of salvation" (2 Corinthians 6:2). "Today if ye will hear His voice, harden not your hearts" (Hebrews 3:7-8). God looks not on outward appearances but on the heart, with its conflicting emotions and hidden impurities (1 Samuel 16:7). He knows its motives and purposes.

Like the psalmist, open your heart to God's all-seeing eye, praying, "Search me, O God, and know my heart: try me, and know my thoughts: and see if there be any wicked way in me, and lead me in the way everlasting" (Psalm 139:23-24). God woos His erring children with tender love, more patient than any earthly parent. His promises and warnings are expressions of His unutterable love. When Satan accuses you of being too sinful, look to your Redeemer and speak of His merits. Acknowledge your sin but declare, "Christ Jesus came into the world to save sinners" (1 Timothy 1:15), and through His matchless love, you can be saved.

Jesus illustrated this with the parable of two debtors—one owing a small sum, the other a great debt—both forgiven by their lord. When asked which debtor would love their lord more, Simon answered, "He, to whom he forgave most" (Luke 7:43). Those who are forgiven much will love Christ most and stand nearest to His throne, praising Him for His great love and infinite sacrifice. The fuller our understanding of God's love, the deeper our realization of sin's gravity, melting our hearts with tenderness and contrition.

Confess both your hidden and visible sins. "He that covereth his sins shall not prosper: but whoso confesseth and forsaketh them shall have mercy" (Proverbs 28:13). The Apostle James urges, "Confess your faults one to another, and pray one for another, that ye may be healed" (James 5:16). Confess your sins to God, who alone can forgive, and your faults to one another, seeking His mercy and grace.

WORDS OF GENUINE CONVERSION

1.   "He who truly serves Me desires to sin no more. He disciplines his body, guards his speech, and speaks only when necessary or to praise his Creator."

2.   Guard your body carefully, for it is weak and prone to sin, which can lead the soul to destruction.

3.   Do not indulge your body's desires but keep it in check through discipline and self-denial to overcome temptations that seek to destroy you.

4.   Live and watch over your body in such a way that you may rejoice forever in eternity.

5.   Those who resolve to walk My path will be strengthened and led to heavenly splendor. I will grant them grace to discern between good and evil on their journey to eternity.

6.   Silence helps overcome sin. Speak little, and when speech is unnecessary, remain silent, pray, and contemplate Me.

7.   Avoid long conversations, for they are traps set by the devil to ensnare many souls.

8.   On fasting days, practice abstinence and discipline your body for your sins. "By denying yourself food, you will gain greater merit in My eyes."

9.   Pray without ceasing so that your soul remains in constant communion with Me.

10.   Call evil what it is—evil—so that your days may be long, as it is written.

CHOOSE THE WAY TO HEAVEN

Consider these words carefully and choose the path to eternal life. Jesus declared, "I am the way, the truth, and the life. No one comes to the Father except through Me" (John 14:6). Now is the time of God's favor; now is the day of salvation (2 Corinthians 6:2).

— Yoursoulriter

CHAPTER 3:

PLACE GOD FIRST

God must be central in all we do, for He is the Creator of the universe, the everlasting Redeemer whose "yes" is yes and whose "no" is no. Brethren, those who walk with God follow the right path in life. If you place Him last, He becomes last in your life; but if you place Him first, He becomes all in all. Amen.

Human wisdom and skill cannot produce life in even the smallest object in nature. Only through the life God imparts can plants or animals thrive. Likewise, spiritual life is born in the hearts of men only through God's power. Unless a person is "born from above," they cannot partake in the life Christ came to give (John 3:3, margin). Just as God's power causes the seed to develop—"first the blade, then the ear, after that the full corn in the ear" (Mark 4:28)—so too does His grace sustain spiritual growth.

Through the matchless gift of His Son, God has enveloped the world in an atmosphere of grace as tangible as the air we breathe. All who choose to inhale this life-giving grace will live and grow into the fullness of Christ Jesus. Jesus taught, "Abide in Me, and I in you. As the branch cannot bear fruit of itself, except it abide

in the vine; no more can ye, except ye abide in Me...
Without Me ye can do nothing" (John 15:4–5). J

ust as a branch depends on the vine for growth and fruitfulness, you are wholly dependent on Christ to live a holy life. Abiding in Him, you will flourish, drawing life from Him to resist temptation and grow in grace. Like a tree planted by rivers of water, you will not wither but bear fruit.

Some believe in God only for forgiveness of sins, thinking they can stand alone in their endeavors. Woe to them, for Christ says, "Without Me ye can do nothing." We must abide in Christ daily, hourly, ceaselessly. He is not only the author but the finisher of our faith (Hebrews 12:2).

Christ must be first, last, and always, present at every step of the way. David declared, "I have set the Lord always before me: because He is at my right hand, I shall not be moved" (Psalm 16:8).

HOW AM I TO ABIDE IN CHRIST?

Abide in Christ as you first received Him: "As ye have therefore received Christ Jesus the Lord, so walk ye in Him" (Colossians 2:6). "The just shall live by faith" (Hebrews 10:38). You gave yourself wholly to God, to serve and obey Him, accepting Christ as your Savior. You could not atone for your sins or change your heart, but by faith, you trusted God to do this for Christ's sake.

By faith, you became Christ's, and by faith, you must grow in Him—giving and taking. Give all—your heart, will, and service—to obey His requirements. Take all—Christ, the fullness of all blessings—to abide in your heart as your strength, righteousness, and everlasting helper, empowering you to obey.

Consecrate yourself to God each morning as your first act. Pray, "Take me, O Lord, as wholly Thine. I lay all my plans at Thy feet. Use me today in Thy service. Abide with me, and let all my work be wrought in Thee." Surrender your plans daily to Him, and He will abide with you. Day by day, entrust your life to God, and it will be molded more and more into the likeness of Christ.

God is the source of life, light, and joy for the universe. Like rays of light from the sun or streams bursting from a spring, blessings flow from Him to all His creatures. When God's life fills your heart, His love and blessings will flow through you to others.

WHY, O MAN, DO YOU RAISE YOUR HEAD?

Why, O man, do you stand with head held high, boasting of your achievements? Who gave you memory, intelligence, willpower, industry, and virtues? Who created your body's organs, which faithfully obey their Creator's commands, enabling the lifeless earth to move, work, see, hear, and choose between good and evil? All of nature and its fruits—sweet and bitter—come from Me. I control you, O mortal man. If you have done good, My encouragement enabled you; if evil, the devil seduced you. No one acts alone. The good are guided by My grace, while the evil are led down dark paths by the devil.

All treasures you possess are Mine, given to you to use for good or ill. I entrusted My treasures to you, My creature, so you should not boast. All praise belongs to the Lord of heaven for every gift received!

Man is among God's most beloved creatures, so we must place Him first in all we do, even in our hearts, for He placed us first among all creation. Let us honor God as He has honored us, that we may sit with Him on His throne. Amen.

In the spiritual realm, as we meditate on God's words of love, His Spirit fills our hearts and minds, transforming selfish attitudes and fretfulness. "Let the word of Christ dwell in you richly" (Colossians 3:16).

When we invite God to be first and last in our lives, we experience the peace and servanthood that characterized Christ's life. Jesus must be our daily focus. By letting our Savior live through us, others will see Christ in our actions. Spend time in God's Word today, that His love may shine through you. Pray, "Give us, O Lord, a strong desire to seek Your Word each day. Help us hide it in our hearts, lest we stray from its truth" (Yoursoulriter). Amen.

Knowing God is the key to eternal life. A life in Christ is one of restfulness—not ecstatic feelings, but abiding peace through trust in Him. Your hope lies not in yourself but in Christ—your weakness united to His strength, your ignorance to His wisdom, your frailty to His enduring might. Do not focus on self but on Christ's love, self-denial, humility, purity, holiness, and matchless character. By loving Him, imitating Him, and depending wholly on Him, you will be transformed into His likeness. Place Him first in all you do, and He will abide in you. Amen.

Like the disciples, who were "subject to like passions as we are" (James 5:17), we face the same battle with sin and need the same grace to live a holy life. Reflect: Are you a disciple placing God first?

— Yoursoulriter

CHAPTER 4:

GOD MADE

In Genesis, the Bible reveals that God created man in His own image (Genesis 1:27). We are God-made, crafted for His purpose and placed above all earthly creation. God declares, "I love My people and have given them everything, that they might serve Me and come to Me. In My great generosity, I adorned their souls with numerous gifts. Yet many have distorted My image, forgetting their origin and destiny. They are overly anxious about their lives and fail to recognize that all they possess comes from My hand. Those entrusted with greater gifts bear greater responsibility for how they use them. Those with less are still accountable to My word. The sun warms the earth, the rain waters the plains—everything grows through Me, and without Me, nothing can live on, under, or above the earth."

Sadly, prayer has faded from the lives of many of God's sons and daughters. Even sadder, they have forgotten that I am their God, the Judge of the living and the dead. They eat the food I provide to strengthen their bodies, rest, and rise to a new day, yet many fail to give Me the honor due for all they have received. Christ came to prove His love, making us fully God's own. "If you knew Me better, you would rejoice above all creation and love Me more in everything. Every created thing would whisper to your heart that I care deeply for you. Amen. You would yearn for Me as I yearn for you, and My love would dwell among you on earth. You would live in My blessing and receive My gifts in fullest measure."

Those who live according to My commandments can expect in heaven what no human heart on earth has fully conceived—heavenly peace, beauty, and divine righteousness. I have prepared glorious dwellings for My faithful servants. My beloved, make room in your heart for Me, that I may dwell there for eternity. I delight in a pure and obedient heart and listen attentively to its voice. Yet I find few hearts filled with love, welcoming My presence with gratitude.

God created us to reflect His likeness, so, brethren, do not neglect your soul. On earth, you are pilgrims journeying toward heaven. Live according to His commandments, that you may dwell with Him forever in the place He has prepared. Many do not know Me; some have heard of Me but do not understand; others care nothing for their salvation, living selfishly and trifling with their souls. Darkness has fallen on many, and few walk in the light, zealously fulfilling My desires and striving to lead others to My grace. I pity those who disregard their salvation, wandering in darkness though they live so near the light.

I also pity My children who are ashamed of Me. I will, in turn, be ashamed of them when they stand before Me to be judged according to their works (Mark 8:38).

Brethren, do not presume to place yourself in God's position. If you were God and your child disobeyed, you might punish them harshly. But God is patient, enduring, and forgiving of our sins. Do not place yourself above Him, for He is the merciful Creator.

It is futile for a man to lose his soul, for all the world's wealth cannot redeem it. A soul is more precious than all earthly treasures, which is why the devil lies in wait to destroy it, seeking to ensnare it for hell. When the soul departs from the body, a person sees their misdeeds, but it is too late to save their soul. Work with God's grace from youth, not merely in the hour of death, for then there is no time. As the body craves physical food, the soul hungers for its invisible Creator and Bridegroom. From the womb, the soul joins the body to form a new human life; in death, it returns to God, taking only its good and evil deeds. Those who love Me will live according to My laws. Hell is filled with those who rejected Me and My will.

I did not create you for hell but for Myself. Worship is the foremost duty of all creatures, serving God to save your soul. All other activities are secondary. I created the earth for man, not man for the earth. Pray and work, that I may bless your efforts. Work without prayer is insufficient, and prayer without work is incomplete. "He who will not work, neither should he eat," for he is unworthy of My gifts (2 Thessalonians 3:10).

The Lord desires obedience from all His sons and daughters. Jesus says, "My peace I give unto you: not as the world giveth, give I unto you. Let not your heart be troubled, neither let it be afraid" (John 14:27). "These things have I spoken unto you, that My joy might remain in you, and that your joy might be full" (John 15:11). "Come, ye blessed of My Father, inherit the kingdom prepared for you from the foundation of the world" (Matthew 25:34). Blessed are those who hear and obey. Brethren, know that we are God-made for eternity.

— Yoursoulriter

CHAPTER 5:

LIFE OF A CHRISTIAN

A Christian is a living sermon. "In all things showing yourself to be a pattern of good works" (Titus 2:7). Christians must walk in accordance with God's will, as their lives are meant to be exemplary. The closer you walk with God, the less room there is for anything to come between you and Him. "Enoch walked with God; and he was not, for God took him" (Genesis 5:24).

We know little about Enoch's life—he likely tended herds, worked the land, and cared for his family. Yet, we know he maintained an ongoing conversation with God, expressing his joys, hurts, confusions, and responsibilities for his children. Enoch loved what God loves and hated what God hates. Remarkably, God was pleased with Enoch (Hebrews 11:5).

One day, God may have said, "Enoch, we've come a long way together; why don't you come home and stay with me?" The ancient writer simply states, "And he was not, for God took him" (Genesis 5:24). The Lord still seeks those who will walk with Him. What a privilege for us! The Creator of the cosmos, Ruler of heaven, and Redeemer of mankind seeks our friendship. As Christians, are we seeking His?

"Savior, let me walk beside Thee, let me show Your shadow in me, let me know the joy of walking in Thy strength and not in mine."

— Yoursoulriter.

THE VICTORIOUS LIFE

God desires and commands all believers to live a victorious life. The Christian life begins with God's power: "But as many as received Him, to them He gave the power to become sons of God, even to those who believe in His name" (John 1:12). It is sustained by the same power: "Who are kept by the power of God through faith for salvation ready to be revealed in the last time" (1 Peter 1:5).

Throughout Scripture, God's purpose is victorious living for His children, convicting and transforming the careless, sinful world around them. "You are the salt of the earth; but if the salt loses its flavor, how shall it be seasoned? It is then good for nothing but to be thrown out and trampled underfoot by men. You are the light of the world. A city set on a hill cannot be hidden. Let your light so shine before men, that they may see your good works and glorify your Father in heaven" (Matthew 5:13-16).

Many Christians are defeated due to a lack of understanding of God's provisions for victory. "Therefore My people have gone into captivity, because they have no knowledge; their honorable men are famished, and their multitude dried up with thirst" (Isaiah 5:13). Others neglect daily strength through quiet time, personal Bible study, and prayer. There is no way to sustain Christian living without obedience to Scripture. The path of obedience is the path of blessing. No one can forsake God's ways and commandments and maintain a good relationship with Him.

True sons and daughters in God's family love Him and delight in His commandments. Partial obedience is worthless in God's sight. Those who select some commandments to obey while rejecting others are regarded as rebels, sinners, and enemies of God. "Then I shall not be ashamed, when I have respect for all Your commandments" (Psalm 119:6). "I have esteemed all Your precepts concerning all things to be right" (Psalm 119:128). "All that the Lord has said" (Exodus 24:7), "all that is written therein" (Joshua 1:8), and "every word that proceeds from the mouth of God" (Matthew 4:4) must be wholeheartedly obeyed by those who love and worship God.

No one desiring a victorious life over sin, the world, and the flesh can minimize the power of God's Word. Human language cannot fully describe its power. Saving faith, living faith, and conquering faith are produced by God's Word in the heart. The Word converts, cleanses, strengthens, and upholds us in righteousness.

Christians represent Jesus Christ. He has provided everything necessary for our physical and spiritual lives, yet He grants us freedom to choose between good and evil. Christians are called to teach others to turn from evil ways, and God protects His people from destruction on life's false paths. He gave His all: "I also give myself to you every day that your souls, which are the price of my blood, may be saved." Christians must honor God's representatives, as He has placed them in His stead until the world ends. "You must see in them Myself, the living God, because I live in the hearts of My servants and speak to you through their lips. Look, My beloved creatures, I choose Christians to represent Me on earth to do My will."

"Through My chosen ones, I give you great graces; through them, I forgive your sins; at their hands, I come to your hearts; at their pleading, I hear your entreaties and help you in various concerns. When your soul leaves your body and prepares for its journey to Me in eternity, they bring Me to you as viaticum. Through the prayers of My servants, I look with pity on you,

My creatures! I give you grace because I love you! You can always hear Me through the lips of My chosen servants, great and small." Thus says the Lord. Christians must live so that others are transformed through their character and footsteps. Brethren, strive to be victorious Christians, that your souls may be saved. Amen.

WORD OF LIFE

"Blessed are the poor in spirit, for theirs is the kingdom of heaven" (**Matthew 5:3**).

Jesus began His public ministry by inviting people to conversion, announcing that the kingdom of God is at hand, and healing souls of illness and infirmity. Crowds followed Him. He went up a mountain and taught those around Him, delivering what is known as the "Sermon on the Mount." The novelty of Jesus' message is evident in His first words, proclaiming blessedness not for the rich, powerful, or influential, but for the poor, humble, small, and pure of heart—those who mourn and are oppressed.

This overturns common societal values that exalt consumerism, hedonism, and prestige. Jesus' "good news" brings joy and hope to the least, instilling trust in God's love, which is close to those enduring trials and suffering. This message of joy and salvation is encapsulated in the first of the eight Beatitudes, promising the kingdom of heaven to the poor in spirit.

What does it mean to be poor in spirit? It means being detached from goods, possessions, people, and even oneself—putting aside self to be open to God's will and to love neighbors as we should. It involves willingness to leave everything—father, mother, fields, or country—if God requires it. An example of failing to be poor in spirit is neglecting to feed the spirit with its rightful nourishment, causing it to weaken.

To be "poor in spirit" means trusting not in riches but in God's love and providence. Often, we are "rich" with worries about health, anxiety for relatives, concerns over jobs, uncertainty about actions, or fear of the future. These can block us from seeing clearly, preventing openness to God and others. In these moments, the "poor in spirit" trust in God's love, casting all worries upon Him and experiencing His fatherly care.

We are "poor in spirit" when we are guided by love for others, sharing our time, goods, and capabilities with those in need. By giving everything out of love, we become poor—empty, free, and pure of heart. This poverty and trust become a source of love: because we are empty of ourselves, we can fully welcome God's will and every person we meet as true Christians. Jesus guarantees the kingdom of heaven to those who live with this purity of heart and poverty of spirit—they are blessed.

"For theirs is the kingdom of heaven."

The kingdom of heaven cannot be purchased with riches or conquered with power; it is received as a gift. Jesus asks us to be like children or the poor, who, like children, rely on others for everything. The Holy Spirit, attracted by this emptiness of love, fills our souls without obstacles to full communion. The "poor in spirit" have everything because they keep nothing for themselves; they are poor of themselves and rich with God. The Gospel applies here: "Give, and it will be given to you" (Luke 6:38). We give what we have, and we receive nothing less than the kingdom of heaven.

As Christians, the kingdom of God is already ours if we discern good from evil, hate what God hates, and love what He loves, as Enoch did. Many blessings will be added unto you. Amen. Christians must always remember that the kingdom of heaven is our ultimate destination after our time on earth.

CHAPTER 6:

FRIENDS WE WALK WITH

Who is a friend? A friend knows everything about you—both good and bad—corrects the bad, and still wants to be with you. A true friend sticks by you in pain when others flee. A bad friend deceives you, seeks only personal gain, and abandons you in need.

In friendship, we don't find friends; we make them. The worst enemy you can have is a friend, as they hold the key to your life through trust. Trust only God, not any creature. "Your body has good friends who lead and direct you to heaven, but only a few of My sons and daughters have the will to keep their company: they are solitude, composure, and silence."

Making heaven lies in your hands, so don't let friends mislead you. Choose your friends wisely to avoid being led astray. "In all your ways acknowledge Him, and He shall direct your paths" (Proverbs 3:6). Solitude, composure, and silence have a profound impact on human life. A quiet person is great and can guard secrets. Speaking carelessly makes you vulnerable to destruction. Always walk with those who share your vision and mission.

— Yoursoulriter.

CHAPTER 7:

OVERCOMING TEMPTATION

Certainty of Temptation

After conversion and a decision to serve God, every Christian must understand that temptation is inevitable. Satan, the enemy of our soul, fights to make believers fall from faith in Jesus Christ. Temptation is nearly as old as humanity, and no one is exempt from its challenges, as it is a battle with Satan. Sinners, however, are free from temptation because they are already dead in sin and aligned with the devil (1 John 3:8). Temptation comes from Satan to lure believers back into sin.

1. Definition of Temptation: Temptation is an urge— whether internal or external—induced by Satan to act contrary to God's will and fall from faith. It can also be a suggestion to do evil.

2. Revelations About Temptation: Temptation is not sin, but yielding to it is. Jesus was tempted by Satan yet remained sinless because He resisted (2 Corinthians 5:21; Proverbs 1:10).

3. Inevitability: Temptation is an unavoidable encounter in the Christian race, as Jesus Himself was tempted (Luke 4:2-12).

4. Growth Through Overcoming: Each temptation overcome elevates you spiritually (John 15:2).

5. God's Plan: God desires believers to overcome all temptations (1 Corinthians 10:13).

6. Sufficient Grace: God's grace is sufficient for every believer (2 Corinthians 12:9; Hebrews 2:18).

Therefore, brethren, be fully determined to overcome all temptations through Christ's strength.

Sources and Causes of Temptation

Scripture reveals that temptation is a common encounter in the Christian pilgrimage, as Jesus Himself overcame temptation (Hebrews 2:18). Before addressing how to overcome temptation, we must understand its sources and causes:

1. Lack of Regular Fellowship with God: "Not forsaking the assembling of ourselves together, as is the manner of some, but exhorting one another, and so much the more as you see the Day approaching" (Hebrews 10:25). Neglecting fellowship—such as daily quiet time, regular Bible study, and church attendance—creates a vacuum that invites temptation (2 Timothy 2:15; Romans 12:2).

2. Unbroken Bridges of Sin: After salvation, believers must destroy sinful influences, such as

immoral clothing, pornographic materials (magazines, films, novels), ungodly love for money, or occultist books (Acts 19:19). "The graven images of their gods you shall burn with fire. You shall not covet the silver or gold that is on them, nor take it for yourselves, lest you be snared by it; for it is an abomination to the Lord your God" (Deuteronomy 7:25). Destroy these to avoid being drawn back into sin.

3. Evil Companionship: "Do not be deceived: 'Evil company corrupts good habits'" (1 Corinthians 15:33). Intimate friendships with evildoers tempt believers to fall. God warns against such relationships to prevent temptation.

4. Evil Thoughts: The heart is "desperately wicked" (Jeremiah 17:9), and evil thoughts are a source of temptation, including lust of the flesh, lust of the eyes, and pride of life (Matthew 15:19; Genesis 6:5; Mark 7:21-23; Proverbs 6:18). What you see influences what you think, so guard your mind.

5. Seeing: Being in the wrong place leads to seeing things that tempt, such as pornographic images, immoral films, or idolatrous practices (2 Samuel 11:1-4). Believers must flee all appearances of evil (1 Thessalonians 5:22; 1 Peter 2:11).

6. Evil Association: "Blessed is the man who walks not in the counsel of the ungodly, nor stands in

the path of sinners, nor sits in the seat of the scornful" (Psalm 1:1). Continuing with sinful associates after salvation invites temptation through their practices (e.g., drinking, immorality, smoking). "Make no friendship with an angry man, and with a furious man do not go, lest you learn his ways and set a snare for your soul" (Proverbs 22:24-25). Evil associations are traps that can wound believers and draw them back to sin (Joshua 23:13).

How to Overcome Temptation

To overcome temptation, believers must master these biblical principles by God's grace:

1. Sound Knowledge of God's Word: Jesus overcame Satan with Scripture (Luke 4:5-8). Unlike Adam and Eve, who fell due to a lack of conviction in God's Word, believers must take God's Word at face value and stand firm.

2. Take Heed: Sin originates in the heart. Believers must arrest sinful thoughts early, consecrating their hearts to God and filling them with His truth.

3. Consecration and Prayer: Since temptation comes from Satan (James 1:13), believers must pray continuously, pulling down strongholds of lust and the flesh. "Walk in the Spirit, and you shall not fulfill the lust of the flesh" (Galatians

5:16). Set your affection on things above and pray without ceasing (2 Corinthians 10:4-5).

4. Watch and Pray: "Watch and pray, lest you enter into temptation. The spirit indeed is willing, but the flesh is weak" (Matthew 26:41). Vigilance and prayer are essential, as the flesh has led many astray. Continuous prayer prepares us for Christ's return.

CHAPTER 8:

CROWNS FOR OVERCOMERS

Scripture promises crowns for those who persevere in Christ:

- Crown of Glory: "When the Chief Shepherd appears, you will receive the crown of glory that does not fade away" (1 Peter 5:4).

- Incorruptible Crown: "Everyone who competes for the prize is temperate in all things. They do it to obtain a perishable crown, but we for an imperishable crown" (1 Corinthians 9:25).

- Crown of Righteousness: "The crown of righteousness, which the Lord, the righteous Judge, will give me on that Day, and not to me only but also to all who have loved His appearing" (2 Timothy 4:8).

- Crown of Life: "Blessed is the man who endures temptation; for when he is tried, he will receive the crown of life which the Lord has promised to those who love Him" (James 1:12).

- Personal Crown: "Behold, I am coming quickly! Hold fast what you have, that no one may take your crown" (Revelation 3:11).

Arise, break up your fallow ground, and fight the good fight of faith so no one takes your crown.

CHAPTER 9:

PATH OF SALVATION

Salvation comes through Jesus Christ, God's only begotten Son, who died to pay the debt of our sins, a debt we could not pay. He suffered on the cross to grant us freedom and peace. Jesus is the way to salvation. To be saved:

1. Accept Him as Your Personal Lord and Savior.

2. Confess All Your Sins to Him.

3. Get to Know Him More.

4. Have a Heart of Forgiveness.

5. Have a Heart of Love.

When we accept Christ, our old life passes away, and we embrace a new life. "Therefore, if anyone is in Christ, he is a new creation; old things have passed away; behold, all things have become new" (2 Corinthians 5:17, NIV). Confess your sins, no matter how unspeakable, for God says, "Come now, and let us reason together," says the Lord. "Though your sins are like scarlet, they shall be as white as snow; though they are red like crimson, they shall be as wool" (Isaiah 1:18, NIV). He desires you to come as you are, and He will cleanse and restore you.

After accepting and confessing, spend time with God to build a strong relationship. Many Christians lack this, making them vulnerable to temptation. Time with God brings peace, joy, and love—gifts no human can provide. A Christian should be surrounded by peace, love, and joy, yet many miss God's blessings by prioritizing worldly pursuits.

Christ calls us to forgive, even those who have deeply hurt us. Forgiveness is the key to happiness and progress. "If you do not forgive, you cannot move forward." He also commands us to love: "The second is this: 'You shall love your neighbor as yourself.' There is no other commandment greater than these" (Mark 12:31). Love those around you, including enemies, and pray for them as an act of love.

RETURN TO THE ALTAR

There is a cry echoing from Heaven—a cry not of judgment, but of longing. "Return to Me," says the Lord, "for I have loved you with an everlasting love." Yet we have strayed. We have traded holy fire for comfort, truth for applause, consecration for convenience.

The altar of our hearts lies broken, unattended, buried beneath the rubble of distractions and delayed obedience. But even now, grace calls. God is not seeking perfection—He is seeking surrender. He is not looking for eloquent prayers—He is searching for broken spirits, humbled hearts, and yielded lives. In every generation, there is a remnant. A people not swayed by culture, but moved by His presence. Will you be among them?

This chapter is not just an invitation. It is a summons. A call to return. To rebuild the altar. To tear down every idol you've allowed to rise in the holy place. To climb again. To burn again. To weep again before the Lord. He Waits at the Altar Before the foundation of the earth, He chose you. While you were still lost, He pursued you. While you were in the pigpen of sin, He prepared a ring and robe. You were never forgotten. He has waited—patiently, lovingly—at the altar of your return. Will you come?

Not tomorrow. Not after another failed plan or heartbreak. Now. The altar is not made of gold, but of surrender. It is not built with stones, but with tears. It is lit not with matches, but with repentance. A Holy Confrontation This is not just a chapter, it is a mirror. Look into it. Are you truly walking with God, or merely walking in the memory of when you once did? Do your lips say "Lord," but your heart is far from Him? Have you allowed the fire to die down while still carrying the appearance of the flame? God is not mocked. And yet, He is merciful. He knocks—not to condemn, but to cleanse.

He wounds—not to destroy, but to heal. He prunes—not

to punish, but so you might bear fruit that remains. Return.

The Ladder to Life Ends Here, But Your Climb Must Continue

You've read the pages. You've heard the call. Now it's time to live it. Get up from where you are. Fall on your knees. Ask for nothing. Offer everything. Let your life be an altar. Let your words be worship. Let your obedience be the fragrance that reaches Heaven. This is your moment. This is your chapter. Return to the altar. God is waiting. "This is not the end of your story. It's the beginning of your climb. God is not asking for perfection—He is calling you higher."

— Yoursoulriter, The Ladder to Life

TEARS TO OIL: A PRAYER
OF RETURN AND REVIVAL

Heavenly Father,

I come before You—not with eloquent words, but with a trembling heart. You see me. You know me. You have watched every silent battle, every fall, every cry I tried to hide. I have wondered. I have delayed.

I have given pieces of myself to things that could never satisfy. But here I am... returning. Let these tears speak what my mouth cannot. Let them fall upon the altar of my heart and become oil in Your hands. Break me where I've been hard. Cleanse me where I've been compromised.

Restore to me the awe of Your presence. I don't want to just read about fire—I want to burn for You again. Father, rekindle the flame. Let every dry place in me drink deeply of Your Spirit. Let the noise of this world grow faint as I sit at Your feet again. Strip away every idol. Silence every lie. Remove everything that numbs me to You.

I lay down my will. I lay down my timeline. I lay down the version of me I tried to build without You. Now, God of Abraham, Isaac, and Jacob—God of my soul—Have Your way. If You want my pain, take it. If You want my dreams, take them. If You want my future, it's Yours.

Let my obedience be the oil You pour out. Let my life become a song of worship. Let my name be forgotten—so long as Yours is glorified. I don't want the world. I want You. I don't want popularity—I want purity. I don't want platforms, I want presence. I don't want momentary power—I want eternal purpose. So here I am, Abba— Broken. Willing. Returning. Anoint me afresh. Fill me again. Use me completely. From this day forward, let my life be the altar, and my heart the sacrifice. May every tear I've cried become oil You pour into others. And may The Ladder to Life become a legacy of surrender. In the mighty, matchless, resurrected name of Jesus Christ—Amen

"True revival doesn't begin in the church—it begins on the altar of a surrendered heart. When your tears become prayers and your pain becomes purpose, Heaven responds. The climb to life begins where your will ends."

— Yoursoulriter, The Ladder to Life

CHAPTER 10:

TEN REASONS TO BELIEVE IN THE CHRISTIAN FAITH

1. Its Explanations for Life: Christianity reflects the caring attention evident in nature's species and ecosystems (Psalm 19:1-6; Romans 1:16-25). Christ reveals a God who cares deeply, clothing Himself in humanity to suffer and die for us.

2. Its Foundational Claim: The first Christians witnessed Jesus' crucifixion, burial, and resurrection. They risked their lives proclaiming He was alive after three days (Acts 2:22-24).

3. Its Analysis of Human Nature: The Bible identifies the heart as the source of society's problems, listing sins like evil thoughts, murders, and thefts (Matthew 15:19-20).

4. Its Impact on Society: Jesus, a carpenter from Nazareth, transformed the world. Calendars, Western values, scientific methodology, and social relief agencies stem from biblical principles.

5. The Credibility of Its Founder: Jesus claimed to come from heaven, fulfill prophecy, and die for sins. His miracles and sinless life led His disciples

to declare, "We have come to believe and know that You are the Christ, the Son of the living God" (John 6:69).

6. The Reliability of Its Book: Written over 1,600 years by 40 authors, the Bible's historical and geographical accuracy is supported by archaeology, including the Dead Sea Scrolls, and its prophetic accuracy remains compelling.

7. Its Continuity with the Past: Jesus fulfilled the Old Testament sacrificial system and God's promise to Abraham, making Christianity one continuous story from Genesis to Revelation (Acts 2:22-39; 1 Corinthians 15:1-8).

8. Its Power to Change Lives: From Paul's transformation to countless others, lives are changed by Christ's cleansing and justification (1 Corinthians 6:11; Galatians 1:11-24).

9. Its View of Human Achievement: Despite human efforts, wars, diseases, and spiritual deception persist, as predicted (Matthew 24:5-31; 2 Timothy 3:1-5).

10. Its Offer of Salvation: Salvation is a gift received through faith in Christ, not earned by works, offering forgiveness and eternal life (Romans 10:9-13; Ephesians 2:8-10).

CHAPTER 11:

STEPS TO KNOWING GOD

1. Recognize God Loves You: "For God so loved the world that He gave His only begotten Son, that whoever believes in Him should not perish but have everlasting life" (John 3:16).

2. Admit You Need Help: "Men loved darkness rather than light, because their deeds were evil" (John 3:19).

3. Believe Jesus Is the Only Savior: "Behold, the Lamb of God who takes away the sin of the world!" (John 1:29).

4. Receive Jesus as Your Savior: "But as many as received Him, to them He gave the right to become children of God" (John 1:12).

5. Acknowledge Jesus as Lord and Friend: "You are My friends if you do whatever I command you" (John 15:14).

6. Recognize You Belong to God's Family—the Church: "I am the vine, you are the branches" (John 15:5).

7. Commit to Serve the Lord: Pray, read the Bible, and witness (John 14:13; John 8:31-32; John 20:21).

Prayer of Commitment:

Heavenly Father, I know I have sinned and need Your forgiveness. I believe Your Son, Jesus Christ, died for me on the cross, and I am willing to repent and turn from my sins. I now invite Jesus to come into my heart and life as my personal Savior, and by Your grace, I am willing to follow and obey Him as the Lord of my life. Amen.

CHAPTER 12:

DEMONSTRATION OF GOD'S POWER IN JUDGMENT

"Then the Lord said to Moses, 'Go to Pharaoh and say to him, "Thus says the Lord: Let My people go, that they may serve Me. But if you refuse to let them go, behold, I will plague all your country with frogs. The Nile shall swarm with frogs, which shall come up into your palace, your bedroom, your bed, the houses of your servants, your people, and into your ovens and kneading bowls. The frogs shall come up on you, your people, and all your servants"'" (Exodus 8:1-4).

God demonstrated His judgment on Pharaoh for his disobedience. When we disobey God, knowing our actions are wrong, we allow the "Pharaoh" within us to rule instead of submitting to the Creator. Every Pharaoh controlling your life is destroyed in Jesus' name. Amen.

CONCLUSION

This book, brought by His sufficient grace, is not merely for reading or keeping but contains the truth about God. Knowing and obeying God's Word brings light, wisdom, and understanding (Job 28:12-28). Brethren, accept Christ while you are young; it's never too late. Follow His ways to avoid being misled. Place Him first in all you do, for He is the Omnipotent Creator who never forgets you. He alone leads to the true way of life. Don't wait for signs, a pastor's call, or calamity to repent. Now is the time to reconcile with your Maker and give your life to Christ. The days of the Lord are near. Avoid the endless torment of hell and let God reside in your heart today!

www.ingramcontent.com/pod-product-compliance
Lightning Source LLC
Chambersburg PA
CBHW051335120626
46547CB00016B/2550